W9-DDH-667

Harriet Beecher Stowe

THE INSPIRING LIFE STORY OF THE
ABOLITION ADVOCATE

BY BRENDA HAUGEN

COMPASS POINT BOOKS
a capstone imprint

Compass Point Books are published by Capstone,
1710 Roe Crest Drive, North Mankato, Minnesota 56003
www.mycapstone.com

Copyright © 2017 by Compass Point Books, a Capstone imprint.
All rights reserved. No part of this publication may be reproduced in whole
or in part, or stored in a retrieval system, or transmitted in any form or by
any means, electronic, mechanical, photocopying, recording, or otherwise,
without written permission of the publisher.

Editorial Credits
Catherine Neitge and Angela Kaelberer, editors; Ashlee Suker, designer;
Wanda Winch, media researcher; Kathy McColley, production specialist

Photo Credits
Alamy: Lebrecht Music and Arts Photo Library, 21, 36; Capstone, 55;
Corbis: Bettmann, 53, Hulton-Deutsch Collection, 19, 58, Phil Schermeister,
99, Swim Ink 2, LLC, 83; Getty Images Inc: Hulton Archive, 79, 93, 105,
Stock Montage, 101; Granger, NYC – All rights reserved, 7, 9, 26, 29,
31, 39, 45, 50, 57, 63, 67, 75, 83, 102, 104 (left); Harriet Beecher Stowe
Center, Hartford, CT, 25, 47, 72, 91, 97; Library of Congress: Prints
and Photographs Division, 70, 81, 84, 87, 88, 94, 104 (right); Newscom:
akg-images, 10, Picture History, 4, 15; North Wind Picture Archives, 41,
103; The Schlesinger Library, Radcliffe Institute, Harvard University,
22; Shutterstock: Everett Historical, 12, 60, gudinny, design background;
SuperStock: Fine Art Images, 35

Library of Congress Cataloging-in-Publication Data
Names: Haugen, Brenda, author.
Title: Harriet Beecher Stowe : the inspiring life story of the abolition
advocate / by Brenda Haugen.
Description: North Mankato, Minnesota : Compass Point Books, an imprint
of Capstone Press, 2017. | Series: CPB grades 4-8. Inspiring stories. |
Includes bibliographical references and index.
Identifiers: LCCN 2016004333
ISBN 9780756551643 (library binding)
ISBN 9780756551865 (ebook (pdf))
Subjects: LCSH: Stowe, Harriet Beecher, 1811-1896—Juvenile literature.
| Women authors, American—19th century—Biography—Juvenile
literature. | Abolitionists—United States—Biography—Juvenile literature.
Classification: LCC PS2956 .H384 2016 | DDC 813/.3 [B]—dc23
LC record available at https://lccn.loc.gov/2016004333

Printed and bound in Canada.
009644F16

Table of Contents

Harriet Beecher Stowe fought the evils of slavery through her writing.

chapter One

A STORY THAT CHANGED THE WORLD

On June 5, 1851, readers of *National Era*, a Washington, D.C., newspaper, found an interesting story in its pages. But it wasn't a news story. It was a novel that told of the plight of a group of African-American slaves in Kentucky. It was called *Uncle Tom's Cabin*. Newspaper readers were hooked. Every week for the next 10 months, they eagerly awaited the next chapter that continued the story of Eliza, Uncle Tom, young Harry, and little Eva. By the time the last chapter was published April 1, 1852, the newspaper's subscribers had increased from about 10,000 to 15,000. The author's name was on everyone's lips: Harriet Beecher Stowe.

When she began writing *Uncle Tom's Cabin* early in 1851, Harriet Beecher Stowe was 39 years old and living in Maine. She was married and the mother of six children. Her youngest child, Samuel Charles, who was nicknamed Charley, had died at the age of 18 months in 1849. Adding to Stowe's grief over the baby's death was her sadness and anger about the issue of slavery.

Slavery had been part of the American colonies since the 1600s. Large farms called plantations were common in the southern states. Plantation crops such as tobacco, rice, and cotton needed many workers to plant, tend, and harvest them. By using unpaid slave labor, plantation owners lowered their production costs. By 1850 more than 3 million slaves lived in the United States.

In September 1850 the U.S. Congress passed five laws that came to be known as the Compromise

UNCLE TOM'S CABIN;

OR,

LIFE AMONG THE LOWLY.

BY

HARRIET BEECHER STOWE.

VOL. I.

ONE HUNDREDTH THOUSAND.

BOSTON:
JOHN P. JEWETT & COMPANY
CLEVELAND, OHIO:
JEWETT, PROCTOR & WORTHINGTON.
1852.

Title page from the 100,000th copy of the first edition of Uncle Tom's Cabin of 1850. The compromise was intended to ease tension between southern slaveholders and northern abolitionists, who wanted to outlaw slavery.

The tension had increased after the Mexican War (1846–1848), which brought new territory into the United States. Southern leaders wanted slavery to be legal in these new territories when they became states. Northern politicians didn't want slavery to spread. Under the Compromise of 1850, California was admitted to the Union as a free state. In the new territories of New Mexico and Utah, settlers would be allowed to vote on whether they would allow slavery.

What upset Stowe most about the compromise was the Fugitive Slave Act. This law required runaway slaves who escaped north to freedom to be returned to their masters in the South. The new law required everyone to help capture runaway slaves or face fines and jail sentences. Stowe felt called upon to show the cruelty of slavery and work to bring it to an end.

Stowe wrote fervent letters to family members about the Fugitive Slave Act. She argued the issue with some

Slaves at risk of running away were forced to wear iron collars.

of her neighbors. She wished she could do more, but she couldn't think of how to help. Her answer came in a letter.

For years, Stowe had helped her family earn a living by writing and selling articles to magazines. One day she received a letter from her brother Edward's wife, Isabella Beecher. Isabella suggested that Harriet use her gift for writing to fight the Fugitive Slave Act.

Harriet Beecher Stowe's writing would make her famous around the world.

"Now, Hattie, if I could use a pen as you can, I would write something that would make this whole nation feel what an accursed thing slavery is," Isabella wrote.

Stowe read Isabella's letter to her children. "I will write something," Stowe declared. "I will if I live." In 1852 her serialized newspaper story was published as a book and became a huge success. *Uncle Tom's Cabin* sold nearly 1 million copies in the United States and Great Britain in its first year of publication. But it was more than an interesting story. Not only did it inform people about the horrors of slavery, it further split an already divided country. President Abraham Lincoln even credited the book as one of the causes of the Civil War.

Stowe quickly became the most famous American woman in the world. She used her fame to spread her message, proving just how mighty the pen can be.

Harriet Beecher Stowe and her brother, Henry Ward Beecher

Chapter Two

A PREACHER'S DAUGHTER

Harriet Elizabeth Beecher was born June 14, 1811, in a frame house in Litchfield, Connecticut. She was the seventh of Lyman and Roxanna Beecher's nine children. She was named after her mother's older sister, Harriet Foote. Her family nicknamed her "Hattie."

Growing up, Harriet was closest to her brother Henry. Although Henry was two years younger than Harriet, people often thought they were twins. Harriet was a tomboy, and she loved playing outdoors with Henry. They fished, hiked, and gathered wood together. In the summer they climbed trees and picked berries. In the winter they sledded down snowy hills.

The two children also sometimes got into trouble together. Their mother, Roxanna, loved flowers and was proud of her beautiful gardens. One day while their mother was away from the house, Harriet and Henry discovered her flower bulbs. She was storing them in the house until it was time to plant them in the spring. Mistaking the bulbs for sweet onions, the children ate every single one. When Roxanna got home, she discovered what Harriet and Henry had done. Instead of yelling at them or punishing them, Roxanna gently explained what they had done wrong.

"My dear children, what you have done makes mamma very sorry," Mrs. Beecher said. "Those were not onions but roots of beautiful flowers, and if you had let them alone we should have next summer in the garden great beautiful red and yellow flowers such as you never saw."

Harriet and Henry were sorry for hurting their mother's feelings and left her bulbs alone after that.

Lyman Beecher (center) with his famous children, Harriet and Henry

While Harriet's mother was quiet and gentle with her children, her father was stern and strict. Lyman Beecher was one of the most famous preachers of his time. When Harriet was growing up, he served as the minister of the First Congregational Church of Litchfield.

Beecher expected much of his children. If they misbehaved during church services, they were sent to bed that night without dinner. He wished for Henry and the other boys in the family to attend college and become preachers. His ambitions for Harriet and her sisters weren't as great. In those days girls seldom had careers. Most either got married and raised families or lived at home with their parents all of their lives. While Beecher believed in education for girls, he didn't think that women could achieve the same things that men could. He sometimes expressed regret about his intelligent youngest daughter. "Hattie is a genius," Lyman once said. "I would give a hundred dollars if she were a boy." That was a lot of money then.

But life in the Beecher household wasn't all work and no play. The family found time to have fun. Harriet's father took the boys hunting and fishing. The family also enjoyed picnics and hayrides.

Beecher also taught his children to appreciate music. The Beechers held family "sings." Older sisters Catharine and Mary played the piano, and brothers

Edward and William joined in on flute. Lyman played the violin, although not very well.

"So we had often domestic concerts, which, if they did not attain to the height of artistic perfection, filled the house with gladness," Harriet remembered.

When Harriet was 5, life changed dramatically for the Beecher family. Mrs. Beecher died September 24, 1816, of tuberculosis. Harriet's oldest sister, 16-year-old Catharine, stepped in to help her father raise the younger children. Lyman would later remarry a woman named Harriet

TUBERCULOSIS

The disease that took Harriet's mother's life was tuberculosis, a bacterial disease that mainly affects the lungs. At the time Harriet's mother had it, people called the disease consumption because its victims became very weak and lost weight.

Before the late 1800s, it was one of the most deadly diseases in the world. It spread when an infected person coughed or sneezed and released the bacteria into the air. Since the 1940s tuberculosis has been treated with antibiotics. But in poorer countries, many people still die of the disease.

Porter and have four more children, Frederick, Isabella, Thomas, and James. Even so, Harriet always considered Catharine more of a mother to her than her stepmother was.

Harriet was very sad after her mother's death. To cheer her up, her aunt Harriet Foote took her to her grandmother Roxanna Foote's farm. The farm, called Nutplains, was near Guilford, Connecticut.

Harriet's grandmother had two African-American servants, Dinah and Harry, who were probably former slaves. Harriet's parents had taught her that all people are equal, but Aunt Harriet ordered Dinah and Harry around. She didn't treat them as well as she treated white people. Harriet realized what her aunt was doing was wrong, and she never forgot it.

Harriet started school shortly before her mother died. She liked school and quickly learned to read. By age 6 Harriet could read well enough to borrow books from her father's library, which included hundreds of volumes. She would often sit in a corner of the library and read while Beecher wrote his sermon for the

The Beecher family posed for a photo in 1850. Standing from left: Thomas, William, Edward, Charles, and Henry; seated from left: Isabella, Catharine, Lyman, Mary, and Harriet; inset: James

week. Most of the books were religious titles written for adults. But Harriet also discovered old copies of *Arabian Nights* and Shakespeare's *The Tempest*. She read them cover to cover.

Harriet entered Litchfield Female Academy in 1819 at age 8. Most students weren't allowed to attend until they were at least 12. The school was different from most girls' schools of the time. Instead of concentrating on needlework, music, and painting, the girls at the academy also studied geography, philosophy, and science. Even though it was a girls' school, several of Harriet's brothers also attended the academy.

At school Harriet discovered that in addition to being a good reader, she had a talent for writing. She wrote compositions every week. Harriet quickly became the top student in her class.

One of Harriet's proudest moments occurred about two years later. Her composition teacher asked Harriet and several other students to write essays for the school exhibition program. The topic was "Can the Immortality of the Soul be Proved by the Light of Nature?" When Harriet's teacher read her essay at the exhibition, Beecher asked the teacher who had written it. The teacher replied, "Your daughter, sir!" as Beecher beamed with pride.

Harriet was thrilled that her father was pleased with her work. She would continue to write for the rest of her life.

NICKNAME:	Hattie
DATE OF BIRTH:	June 14, 1811
BIRTHPLACE:	Litchfield, Connecticut
FATHER:	Lyman Beecher (1775–1863)
MOTHER:	Roxanna Foote Beecher (1775–1816)
EDUCATION:	Attended Litchfield Academy and Hartford Female Seminary
SPOUSE:	Calvin Ellis Stowe (1802–1886)
DATE OF MARRIAGE:	January 6, 1836
CHILDREN:	Harriet (1836–1907) Eliza (1836–1912) Henry (1838–1857) Frederick (1840–presumed dead 1870) Georgianna (1843–1890) Samuel Charles (1848–1849) Charles Edward (1850–1934)
DATE OF DEATH:	July 1, 1896
PLACE OF BURIAL:	Andover, Massachusetts

Harriet and her twin daughters, Harriet (Hattie) and Eliza

Chapter Three

MARRIAGE AND FAMILY LIFE

Thirteen-year-old Harriet packed a bag and left Litchfield for good in September 1824. The year before, her older sisters Catharine and Mary had started the Hartford Female Seminary in nearby Hartford, Connecticut. Harriet lived with a local family and attended classes at the school. She studied Italian, Latin, French, and philosophy. She also served as one of the editors of the school newspaper.

Mary Beecher got married in 1827 and quit teaching at the school. Catharine asked 16-year-old Harriet to take Mary's place. For the next several years, Harriet taught at the school while continuing to take classes.

Harriet enjoyed reading the romantic works of English poet Lord Byron and dreamed of becoming a poet herself. Catharine disagreed, telling Harriet she should concentrate on teaching. Even so, Harriet continued to write, hiding her poetry from her sister. She wrote late at night by candlelight or an oil lamp, a practice she would continue throughout her life.

By age 21, Harriet was teaching full time at Catharine's school. She taught composition and also shared her love of art with the students in her drawing and painting classes.

Lyman Beecher took a new job as president of Lane Theological Seminary in Cincinnati, Ohio, in 1832. Harriet moved to Cincinnati with her father and stepmother, her aunt Esther, her brothers George, Henry, and James, and her sisters Catharine and Isabella. Catharine planned to start a new school, Western Female Institute, in Cincinnati. She asked Harriet to teach at the new school.

The Beecher house in Cincinnati was called Walnut Hill.

Harriet worked hard as a teacher. She got up at 6:00 a.m. to be at the school by 7:00 a.m. She often stayed until late at night to finish all of her work, without any extra pay. The school had a tight budget and often couldn't afford to buy enough textbooks. To help out, Harriet wrote a geography book, *Primary Geography for Children*, which the school used for many years. She earned $187 for it, which was almost as much money as Catharine made in a year.

Harriet discovered that she enjoyed writing much more than teaching. The success of her geography book encouraged her to start another book, *New England Sketches*. This collection of short stories was published in 1835.

Catharine had started two schools, but she didn't really like to teach either. She preferred to set up the school's curriculum and then have others teach the classes. Harriet's lack of interest in teaching and Catharine's pressure on her to work more hours caused disagreements between the sisters.

CATHARINE'S TRAGEDY

Harriet's oldest sister Catherine never married. In her early 20s she became engaged to a young man named Alexander Fisher. Sadly, Fisher died in a shipwreck off the coast of Ireland in 1822. He left Catharine $2,000, which she used to open her first school in Hartford.

Even with all the time Harriet spent working, she found some time for fun. She joined an organization called the Semi-Colon Club. Her uncle Samuel Foote started the club. Its members met each week for learning and fun. They talked about books and also discussed their writing. At each meeting one member would read the stories and articles that the other members had written. Members could either sign their work or submit it anonymously.

Members of the Semi-Colon Club included authors, lawyers, and other important people in Cincinnati. One was Judge James Hall, the editor of *Western Monthly Magazine*. He praised Harriet's writing and published her first story. Hall also encouraged Harriet to send in a short story to a writing competition that his magazine was sponsoring. Harriet's story, "Uncle Lot," won her a prize of $50. That was a lot of money in 1834.

The Semi-Colon members also discussed the issues of the day and what to do about them. One of the most important issues of the time was the question of slavery. Like other members of the Semi-Colon Club, Harriet wanted to end slavery. Her good friend, lawyer Salmon Chase, was a member of the club and active in the antislavery movement.

Harriet also made other friends through the club. They included a young couple just a few years older than she was, Calvin and Eliza Stowe. Calvin worked with Harriet's father as a professor at Lane Theological Seminary. Harriet and Eliza quickly became close friends. But tragically, Eliza became ill from cholera and died in 1834.

Calvin Stowe was overcome with grief after his wife's death. He leaned heavily on the Beecher family. They often invited him to their house for meals. He became especially close with Harriet. She mended his clothes and even fixed his broken glasses. The sorrow they felt over Eliza's death brought Harriet and Calvin closer together. They fell in love and were married January 6, 1836. On September 29 of that year, Harriet gave birth to twin girls. She and Calvin named them Eliza and Harriet.

THE SLAVERY SYSTEM

In the 1700s people thought that slavery might end in the United States. Keeping slaves wasn't cheap, and many people knew slavery was wrong. But those thoughts changed when cotton became a major crop in the South.

Eli Whitney invented the cotton gin in 1793. Whitney's machine made separating cottonseeds from the cotton fibers faster and easier. Farmers no longer had to spend many hours cleaning the cotton by hand. They could now plant much more cotton using slave laborers to do the work.

Another invention also helped the cotton boom. The spinning mule machine quickly spun the cotton into a fine thread. With these inventions, cotton cloth became much cheaper to produce. The demand for cotton increased, which also increased the demand for slave labor.

People were getting rich raising and selling cotton. But cotton wore out the soil quickly. Growers pushed west into Georgia and Alabama in search of richer soil. They took their slaves with them, spreading slavery through the South.

Like Harriet, Calvin was intelligent and had a good sense of humor. He could speak Italian, German, Latin, Hebrew, Greek, Arabic, Spanish, and French. He was an expert in the field of education, and he knew the Bible even better than Harriet's father.

But Calvin wasn't perfect. He tended to be absentminded and fussy. He counted on Harriet to keep him organized. That didn't go well, because Harriet wasn't any more organized than he was. Calvin sometimes had hallucinations. He said he saw mysterious figures coming out of furniture or out of the floor. He also believed he was psychic and could predict events before they happened. Calvin didn't handle stress well. He often just went to bed and stayed there. Harriet had to deal with the problems the family faced on her own.

Life often was a struggle for the Stowe family. During the next 15 years, five more children joined the twin girls—Henry in 1838, Frederick in 1840, Georgianna in 1843, Samuel Charles in 1848, and Charles Edward in 1850. The large family barely

Harriet and Calvin Stowe in the early 1850s

survived on Calvin's small salary. Sometimes they had to get by on even less. The seminary was just getting started, and many times Calvin didn't receive his full paycheck.

Harriet cooked, cleaned, mended clothing, shopped for food, and cared for her children and husband. But she didn't want to be tied down to housework all the time. She continued to write, both for the satisfaction and the money that it brought to the family. In a letter to a friend, she wrote: "If you see my name coming out everywhere—you may be sure of one thing, that I *do* it for the *pay*." Part of the reason she wrote was to be able to afford to hire help to give her *more* time to write. "I have determined not to be a mere domestic slave," wrote Harriet.

WRITING FOR MONEY

Stowe earned about $2 for each page she wrote for magazines. That was a lot of money for the 1830s, especially for a woman. Male factory workers earned about $2 a day, while top-level female workers made about half of that. A farm laborer earned about 75 cents for a 10-hour workday. Unskilled female workers made 35 to 50 cents a day.

Calvin Stowe also believed Harriet's writing was important. He didn't mind the time she spent working on articles. *Godey's Lady's Book,* one of the most respected and popular women's magazines of the time, published several of her stories. Thousands of readers came to recognize Harriet Beecher Stowe's name. In a year's time, Stowe earned about $100, which was enough to hire women to take care of household chores and watch the children. The family remained broke and in debt, though.

Harriet knew she needed to keep writing to support her family. She wrote no matter how tired or ill she was. Once she even wrote at the kitchen table with one of her babies in a clothes basket by her feet. When a cholera outbreak hit Cincinnati in the summer of 1845, an already tired Stowe became very sick. Doctors could do nothing to help her, and it seemed that she would die.

Harriet clung to life as her husband, father, and brothers prayed for her. Slowly she began to recover from the cholera. But by early 1846, it seemed as though she might never return to her full strength. Her sister Catharine urged Harriet to go to a health spa in Brattleboro, Vermont. Friends of the Stowe family agreed to pay for the cost and took over the care of the Stowe children.

The spa's treatment was called a water cure. Patients were wrapped in wet bandages in an effort to release germs and toxins through the pores of the skin.

They also were encouraged to drink lots of water, take long walks in the fresh air, and eat simple, healthy meals. Those things probably helped their recovery much more than the water cure did. Harriet's health began to improve after just a few months at the spa, but she ended up staying there for a year. She wrote to Calvin when her strength began to return:

> *"For this week, I have gone before breakfast to the wave-bath and let all the waves and billows roll over me till every limb ached with cold and my hands would scarcely have feeling enough to dress me. After that I have walked till I was warm, and come home to breakfast with such an appetite! Brown bread and milk are luxuries indeed, and the only fear is that I may eat too much."*

Harriet came home in the spring of 1847 feeling much better than when she had left. In January 1848 she gave birth to her sixth child, Samuel Charles. Nicknamed Charley, the baby was much healthier and easier to care for than her other children had been. This may have been because Harriet herself was in better health during her pregnancy.

Harriet was so pleased with her recovery that she told Calvin a stay at the spa would be good for him as well. Calvin agreed. He left for Brattleboro in June 1848, but didn't plan to stay as long as Harriet did. While he was at the spa, Calvin wouldn't earn

Harriet Beecher Stowe

any money. Harriet would have to keep writing to pay for his treatment. Neither Calvin nor Harriet knew it would be more than a year before they would see one another again.

Harriet Beecher Stowe wrote whenever she could find the time.

Chapter Four

UNCLE
TOM'S CABIN

While Calvin Stowe was in Vermont, another cholera epidemic hit Cincinnati. More than 100 people died of the disease each day. Harriet wrote to Calvin about the horrors of the epidemic:

"Hearse drivers have scarce been allowed to unharness their horses while furniture carts and common vehicles are often employed for the removal of the dead. ... On Tuesday, one hundred and sixteen deaths from cholera were reported, and that night the air was of that peculiarly oppressive, deathly kind that seems to lie like lead on the brain and soul."

Cholera again touched the Stowe family. Harriet remained well, but two of her children, Henry and baby Charley, became sick. Calvin wanted to return home, but Harriet told him to stay in Vermont. She didn't need the responsibility of caring for another sick person.

Henry recovered from his illness. Eighteen-month-old Charley also seemed to be recovering when he suddenly took a turn for the worse. When little Charley died in July 1849, Stowe was heartbroken. She now better understood how women who were slaves felt when their children were sold and they were separated forever.

Calvin returned home after the baby died. Not long after that, he was offered a teaching job at Bowdoin College in Brunswick, Maine. Tired of Cincinnati and their struggles there, he took the job. But he needed to first finish out his teaching contract at the seminary. So in early 1850, Harriet and the children left for Maine without him to get settled.

Henry Ward Beecher offered an enslaved woman for sale to members of his congregation so they could buy her freedom.

Stowe decided to visit friends and family on the trip to Maine. She stopped in Brooklyn, New York, to see her brother Henry Ward Beecher. Henry was a successful minister who actively supported the antislavery movement. He raised money through his church to buy the freedom of slave children and helped the antislavery cause in any way he could.

After a few days in Brooklyn, Stowe headed to Hartford, Connecticut, to see her sisters Mary and Isabella. She then traveled to Boston, Massachusetts, to stay a few days with her brother Edward.

From Boston, Stowe and the children took a steamer to Maine. If Stowe had hoped Maine would be a good change for her family, she quickly changed her mind. A storm was brewing as the steamer made the journey to Maine. The family was grateful to arrive in Brunswick safely, but found that their new house was dreary and damp.

Stowe decided to do whatever she could to make the house into a comfortable home. Even though she was pregnant, she cleaned, papered the walls, and painted the wood floors. In July 1850 her last child, Charles Edward, was born. Also nicknamed Charley, he looked much like the child Stowe had lost. She worried constantly that this Charley would die at an early age as well.

Calvin and Harriet still weren't earning enough money to support their family. That winter, Maine

The Stowe house in Brunswick, Maine

experienced record cold temperatures. Harriet's shoes were full of holes, and she didn't have money for new ones. The Stowes' house was so cold that pails of water froze solid. Harriet and her two oldest daughters sewed quilts to pile on top of the smaller children at night to keep them warm.

Even with all of the problems her family faced, Stowe still found time to write. Her next story was inspired by a vision she had during a church service. In her mind, she saw a black man being beaten by two other black men as a white man urged the two to continue. The beaten man looked at the three others with pity and forgave them. Harriet rushed home from church to write down her story. She didn't have any paper, so she wrote the story on a grocery wrapper.

When she finished, Harriet read the story to her children. They burst into tears. Her sons Henry and Frederick exclaimed, "Oh, mama, slavery is the most cruel thing in the world!" When Calvin read the story, he had the same reaction.

"Hattie," he told Harriet, "this is the climax of that story of slavery you promised sister Katey you would write. Begin at the beginning, and work up to this and you'll have your book."

Harriet remembered her sister-in-law Isabella telling her that she should use her writing talents to tell the world about the evils of slavery. With Calvin's support, Harriet decided to act. During the past year the *National Era* newspaper had published four of her articles. She wrote to the newspaper's editor, Gamaliel Bailey, about her story in March 1851. She told him it would have three or four installments and would be ready in two or three weeks. Bailey agreed to pay her $300 for the finished story.

"I shall show the best side of the thing and something faintly approaching the worst," she said as she began to write *Uncle Tom's Cabin*.

As she began writing, Stowe drew on many memories and stories she had heard over the years. Some came from Eliza Buck, a black woman who worked in the Stowe household as a cook in Cincinnati. Buck had been a slave in Virginia,

A CHANGE OF OPINION

Until she wrote *Uncle Tom's Cabin*, Stowe thought abolitionists were wrong in their approach to the slavery issue. Abolitionists sometimes resorted to violence in their attempt to end slavery. Stowe believed that these acts of violence would only strengthen the southerners' stand against ending slavery. But by the time she finished the book, Stowe considered herself an abolitionist. Yet she never approved of violence as a way to solve a problem.

Louisiana, and Kentucky before she escaped to the North. Buck told Stowe stories about slaves being beaten until they were unconscious and then left in the fields to die. Other enslaved people risked their own lives to sneak down to the fields to help them.

Stowe also thought about the Underground Railroad. This network of people helped escaped slaves and provided safe houses for them to stay on their journey. The Underground Railroad helped thousands of slaves escape through the northern United States into Canada from 1830 to 1860. Because it was so close to slave territory, Cincinnati was an important station on the Underground Railroad. Stowe had known people who had worked on the Underground Railroad when she lived in Ohio.

One of those people was the Reverend John Rankin, a Presbyterian minister who lived in Ripley, Ohio. Rankin's house was on a bluff overlooking the Ohio River. Every night he placed a lit lantern in a window that faced the river. People on the Kentucky side of the river could see the twinkle of the light.

Enslaved people escaped to freedom on the Underground Railroad.

When Harriet, Calvin, and Lyman visited Rankin, they asked him why he put the lantern in the window. He explained that runaway slaves knew the light was a signal. They could stop at his home for food and clothing to help them continue their journey to freedom in Canada.

Harriet listened intently to Rankin's stories about helping escaped slaves. One was about a young mother who crossed the river on winter ice that was beginning to break away. Rankin gave the woman and her baby food and dry clothes before helping them on to another shelter farther north.

Harriet's family also was involved in the Underground Railroad. According to family stories, they helped an African-American servant working in the Stowe home in Cincinnati escape. The woman told Harriet that her old master had come to Cincinnati to force her to return south with him. That night Calvin and Harriet's brother Henry drove the woman to a house on the Underground Railroad.

Uncle Tom's Cabin told the story of several families, but the main character was the slave Uncle Tom. He was an honest, loyal man with a strong religious faith.

When Stowe began her story, she knew it would be the longest thing she had ever written. She didn't realize how long it would take to tell, though. Stowe was literally creating the story as it was being published in the newspaper. Her sisters Catharine and Isabella and her aunt Esther came to help with the

In an illustration from Uncle Tom's Cabin, *a desperate Eliza runs across a frozen river with her son in her arms to keep him from being sold. Artists often depicted Eliza as white, although the character was of mixed race.*

house and children. Still, Stowe missed two deadlines, one in October 1851 and the other in December. The *National Era* had to print an apology to its readers, saying the increasingly popular story would continue in the next issue.

Finally Harriet mailed the last chapter to Bailey. Near the end of the story was the tale that she had originally written on brown grocery paper. Under orders from their evil owner Simon Legree, two male slaves viciously beat Uncle Tom. Uncle Tom forgives the two men before he dies.

"Today I have taken my pen from the last chapter of *Uncle Tom's Cabin* and I think you will understand me when I say that I feel as if I had written some of it almost with my heart's blood," Stowe wrote to Bailey.

John Jewett, a book publisher in Boston, noticed how popular the story was with the *National Era*'s readers. He contacted the Stowes about publishing *Uncle Tom's Cabin* as a book. Jewett offered Harriet half the profits from the book's sales if she agreed to pay for half the cost of printing it. But the Stowes didn't have enough money to risk it on publishing a book. Their friend and business adviser Philip Greeley suggested they take a 10 percent royalty on the book instead of 50 percent. In exchange for a smaller share of the profits, they would ask Jewett to pay all of the book's production costs. Stowe would make less money per book sold, but she wouldn't lose any money if it sold poorly. Jewett agreed.

Stowe didn't have high hopes for *Uncle Tom's Cabin.* She wished she could have taken more time to write the story. She doubted that many copies of the book would sell. She hoped she'd earn at least enough from the book to buy a new silk dress.

Stowe was in for a big surprise. Not only would the book be a huge success, but her name would also be forever linked with the fight to end slavery.

BUSINESS DECISIONS

Harriet lived during a time when women weren't considered as intelligent or capable as men. They weren't even allowed to sign legal contracts. Philip Greeley hadn't read *Uncle Tom's Cabin* when he advised Harriet and Calvin to take just 10 percent of the book royalties. He doubted that a book written by a woman about slavery would interest many people. But once he started reading the book, he couldn't put it down. He said the ending left him in tears. If he had read the book earlier, he might have advised the Stowes to take the riskier deal that would have made them more money.

135,000 SETS, 270,000 VOLUMES SOLD.

UNCLE TOM'S CABIN

FOR SALE HERE.

AN EDITION FOR THE MILLION, COMPLETE IN 1 Vol., PRICE 37 1-2 CENTS.
" " IN GERMAN, IN 1 Vol., PRICE 50 CENTS.
" " IN 2 Vols., CLOTH, 6 PLATES, PRICE $1.50.
SUPERB ILLUSTRATED EDITION, IN 1 Vol., WITH 153 ENGRAVINGS,
PRICES FROM $2.50 TO $5.00.

The Greatest Book of the Age.

Uncle Tom's Cabin *and other writings made Harriet Beecher Stowe a wealthy woman.*

Chapter Three

BIG SUCCESS AND BIG CONTROVERSY

The people who doubted that a novel written by a woman could be successful soon had their answer. Readers snatched up 10,000 copies of *Uncle Tom's Cabin* in the first week after it was published March 20, 1852. Within a year, 300,000 copies of the book were sold. In time, *Uncle Tom's Cabin* would be published in about 40 languages.

Four months after *Uncle Tom's Cabin* was published, the Stowes received the first royalty check—$10,000! It was more money than Calvin could earn in 10 years as a professor. The book helped the Stowes' financial problems, although they still had a hard time managing their money.

But along with the money and praise came criticism and outright anger. *Uncle Tom's Cabin* turned out to be the most controversial book in the history of the United States. People who were against slavery but wanted to preserve the Union were afraid the book would bring about a civil war.

Causing a civil war was the last thing Stowe intended when she wrote *Uncle Tom's Cabin*. Stowe held strong opinions, but she saw herself as someone in the middle of the slavery issue. She wrote the book to paint a true picture of slavery. She wanted readers to sympathize with the black characters and realize that slaves were human beings. She hoped to make northerners understand that it was the system of slavery that was to blame, instead of southern slave owners. She wanted to bring northerners and southerners together to end slavery in a peaceful way. She was sure that if southerners read the book, they'd see how wrong slavery was and that it must end.

Instead, Stowe became a hated person in the South. Southerners thought she was trying to destroy their way of life. Bookstores in the South refused to sell the book. It became dangerous in the South to even own or read a copy of *Uncle Tom's Cabin*. Children in Richmond, Virginia, even had a sidewalk chant that was popular at the time: "Go, go, go, Ol' Harriet

An illustration from an early edition of Uncle Tom's Cabin *featuring Topsy (left) and Eva*

Beecher Stowe! We don't want you here in Virginny. Go, go, go!"

Stowe never expected people to have such strong, emotional reactions to her book. She thought the book might make northerners angry, but was surprised when southerners were upset. She was shocked when southerners called her a radical and a liar. Stowe believed she had shown southerners in a positive way, with more kind masters in the book than cruel ones. After all, the book's most evil character, Simon Legree, was from the North.

Although slavery was legal only in the South, Stowe portrayed it as a national problem in *Uncle Tom's Cabin*. Stowe said northerners were just as much to blame for slavery's continuing existence because they bought cotton and other products from southern plantation owners. Northern bankers, cotton manufacturers, shippers, and others also benefited from the southern economy and its use of slaves. Also, the southern economy depended upon slavery. Stowe believed cruel treatment of slaves had been going on

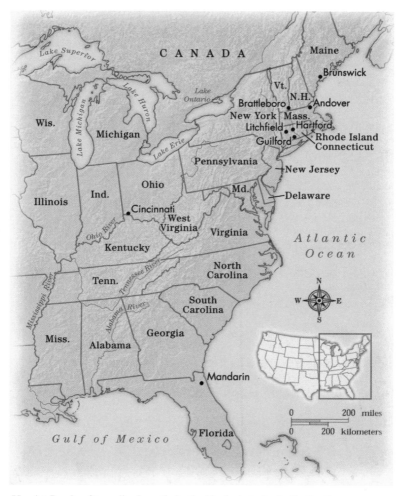

Harriet Beecher Stowe lived mostly in the North, but also in the South.

for so long that violence against slaves wasn't even seen as cruel anymore.

Even though Stowe's father and seven brothers were ministers, she was upset that many U.S. churches didn't take a strong stand on slavery. Instead, they were more likely to condemn minor moral issues such as dancing in public. Stowe believed that if churches across the country united against slavery, it would end. She also thought that by not taking a stand against slavery, churches were actively supporting it.

The northern religious newspaper *New York Observer* agreed with the southerners speaking out against the book. The *Observer* said *Uncle Tom's Cabin* showed a false view of slavery. Its article condemning the book sparked a debate in newspapers across the country. People who thought the book threatened their way of life said it was a book of lies. Those against slavery stood up for Stowe and her book. They also sent her records documenting events much like those in the book.

While it was a work of fiction, Stowe emphasized that her book was based on fact. She was deeply offended that anyone would say otherwise. She followed up *Uncle Tom's Cabin* with an 1853 book titled *The Key to Uncle Tom's Cabin*. It included many

The runaway slave Scipio is hunted by a mob as his master, St. Clare, tries to save him, in an engraving from the first British edition of Uncle Tom's Cabin.

documents and eyewitness accounts proving stories
such as the ones in *Uncle Tom's Cabin* did happen.

Stowe was especially hurt by the criticism of her
book because she had poured so much of herself
into it. "I suffer exquisitely in writing these things. It
may be truly said, I write them with my heart's blood.
Many times in writing *Uncle Tom's Cabin* I thought
my health would fail utterly," wrote Stowe, "but I

The criticism of her book hurt Harriet Beecher Stowe.

prayed earnestly that God would help me till I got through, and still I am pressed beyond measure and above strength."

Stowe began to get threatening letters from southerners. After a while she quit reading the angry letters and answered only the positive ones. But one day a package came to the house that the Stowes couldn't ignore. Calvin opened the package and discovered to his horror that it contained the ear of a slave. The sender warned Harriet that this was what could happen to slaves if she continued to speak out against slavery.

In contrast, reaction in Europe to *Uncle Tom's Cabin* was overwhelmingly positive. In the spring of 1853 the Glasgow Ladies' Anti-Slavery Society and the Glasgow Female New Association for the Abolition of Slavery invited Stowe to make a speaking tour of England and Scotland. The groups would pay the cost of both Harriet and Calvin to make the trip.

Stowe had had enough of dealing with Americans' fury over her book. Even though she wasn't used to public speaking, she agreed to go to Europe. The trip would be the beginning of a new chapter in her life.

Harriet Beecher Stowe received a warm welcome in England.

chapter Six

FAME AND

FORTUNE

Harriet and Calvin Stowe sailed from New York in April 1853 on the clipper ship *Canada*. With them were Harriet's brother Charles; his wife, Sarah; and two relatives of Sarah's. Ten days later the group arrived in Liverpool, England. On the shore was a crowd of people—all there to welcome Harriet.

Stowe was amazed at people's reactions to her once she crossed the ocean. Slavery was illegal in Europe, and *Uncle Tom's Cabin* was hugely popular there. In England the book sold 1.5 million copies the first year it was published. People waited for hours to get a glimpse of Stowe. Huge crowds waited for her at railroad stations, and children brought her bouquets of flowers. People wrote and sang songs about her. All of this unexpected attention left Harriet a bit overwhelmed.

"Nobody expected anything, nobody said anything, and so I wrote freely," Stowe said about writing *Uncle Tom's Cabin*. "Now what embarrasses me is to be announced as an attraction—to have eyes fixed on me and people all waiting."

Harriet had never spoken in front of large groups and wasn't eager to do so. Also, it wasn't considered proper at the time for women to speak in front of audiences that included men. Both Calvin and Charles were used to speaking in public, so they gave most of the speeches on the tour. Harriet shook hands and chatted with people who wanted to meet her. That satisfied her many fans.

Calvin had to return to the United States late in May, but Harriet remained in Europe for five months. She stayed in London for several weeks

An engraving from a drawing by English artist George Richmond

before traveling to France, Switzerland, Germany, and Belgium. Stowe enjoyed experiencing European culture and history. She visited churches and museums. She even became a work of art herself. It took a lot of convincing, but Stowe agreed to allow George Richmond to paint her portrait. He was one of the most famous portrait painters of the time.

"If people really knew me, they wouldn't make such a fuss over me," Stowe told Richmond.

Europeans gave Stowe money for the antislavery movement, as well as gifts. One of her most treasured gifts was a collection of 26 leather-bound books. Women throughout Great Britain and Ireland had circulated a petition asking American women to work together to end slavery in the United States. A total of 562,448 women signed the petition. The signatures were then gathered and printed in the books. The

MEETING THE RICH AND FAMOUS

In Europe Stowe met many famous people, including royalty and well-known authors. At a dinner hosted by the Lord Mayor of London, she sat across the table from author Charles Dickens, whose books are still popular with readers today. Both authors were honored at the dinner for what their writings had done to help poor and disadvantaged people. Stowe often didn't realize the fame of those she met. "I am always finding out, a day or two after, that I have been with somebody very remarkable, and did not know it at the time," she wrote.

books made Stowe feel even better about the work she was doing. And they would come in handy at an important time in U.S. history.

Stowe sailed back to the United States in September 1853. Earlier that year the Stowes had moved to Andover, Massachusetts, when Calvin took a teaching job at Andover Theological Seminary.

Harriet's book royalties helped the large Stowe family live more comfortably. The family used some of the money to remodel a former gymnasium building into their home. The large stone house included a study where Harriet could write uninterrupted every day. Harriet also hired a full-time cook and maid and a part-time laundress.

Stowe needed this household help now more than ever. She received a large sack filled with letters

THE STOWE HOUSE

Harriet and Calvin's large stone home still stands. In 1929 it was moved to its present location on the campus of Phillips Academy, also in Andover. It serves as a dormitory for students at the private high school.

each day. Among the letters were hundreds of offers to speak at various events. Stowe refused the offers, but she did write speeches for other people. In 1856 she published another novel about slavery, *Dred: A Tale of the Dismal Swamp.* Like *Uncle Tom's Cabin,* the book quickly became a bestseller. However, it didn't have the lasting impact that her previous book did.

Stowe also wrote magazine articles supporting the antislavery movement. During the last months of 1853 and all of 1854, she produced an article about every two weeks. The family often hosted antislavery gatherings at their home. Their guests included abolitionist William Lloyd Garrison and former slaves Frederick Douglass and Sojourner Truth, who both worked to end slavery.

Stowe made a second trip to Europe in June 1856. Calvin, her sister Mary, and children Eliza, Hattie, and Henry went with her. The group arrived in Liverpool, England, in mid-July.

Calvin and Henry returned to the United States after a few weeks. Calvin had to get back to his job

An illustration from a 19th century edition of Uncle Tom's Cabin; *the enslaved characters Harry, George, and Eliza would find freedom in Canada.*

at the seminary and 18-year-old Henry was about to start college. Harriet, Mary, and the twins went on to Paris, France. There Harriet spent hours gazing at the paintings in the famous Louvre museum. She also visited a school where she accepted a donation collected by children who had read *Uncle Tom's Cabin*. They wanted the money used to help end slavery.

In Paris, Harriet enrolled her daughters in boarding school. They would remain there for two years. Harriet and Mary then traveled to Italy in February 1857. Their journey was filled with problems. Twice, the wheels fell off their carriage. The carriage driver also kept asking for more money from them to continue the trip. At one point a large group of people surrounded the carriage, also asking for money. Despite these problems, Mary and Harriet arrived safely in Rome. They planned to celebrate Easter in Rome, but a letter from Calvin changed those plans. He hadn't seen his wife for eight months and wanted her to come home.

Before they left Europe, the women went to England to visit Anne Isabella Milbanke. She was the widow of Lord Byron, Harriet's favorite poet. Lady Byron and Stowe had met on Stowe's earlier European trip and had become close friends. Lady Byron was sick in bed when they arrived, but she was happy to see the two women.

GREAT SUCCESS

Stowe had achieved amazing success by 1860. She had more readers than any other U.S. writer, and made more money than any other author. Between 1856 and 1860, Stowe earned about $6,000 each month. At a time when a loaf of bread sold for a penny, that was a huge sum.

But Stowe could have made even more money from her writing. Shortly after *Uncle Tom's Cabin* was published, several playwrights wrote stage plays based on the book. George Aiken's version of the play was the most successful. It ran for nine months at the National Theater on Broadway in New York City. At one point during the 1850s, 16 theater groups were presenting versions of *Uncle Tom's Cabin* on stage. Stowe never bothered to acquire the rights to the play, so she earned nothing from the performances. Other people made a fortune off Stowe's characters.

As they prepared to go home, Stowe had an uneasy feeling. As her ship sailed across the ocean toward the United States, Harriet couldn't shake the feeling that something bad was about to happen.

African-American soldiers served the North with distinction during the Civil War.

chapter seven

THE
COUNTRY
GOES TO WAR

Harriet Beecher Stowe returned to the United States in June 1857. Things were fine at home, but Stowe soon understood the reason for the apprehension she had felt. On July 9 her son Henry drowned while swimming in the Connecticut River in New Hampshire. He had just finished his freshman year at Dartmouth College.

Again the loss of a child sent Stowe into a deep depression. Even worse, Henry had died before fully accepting his religious faith. Everything Stowe knew about religion told her that her son's soul

Henry Ellis Stowe was 19 when he died.

would spend eternity in hell. Over the next two years she turned to writing as a way to deal with her grief. Her novel *The Minister's Wooing* is about a woman grieving the loss of her son. Like Henry, the son died without having a religious conversion. A black woman with a simple faith in God comforts the white woman and reassures her that her son is in heaven. After the book was published in 1859, Stowe returned to her antislavery work.

By that time the disagreements between northern and southern states were increasing. President James Buchanan opposed slavery, but he believed the Constitution protected it.

Abraham Lincoln was elected president in 1860. In his inauguration speech, Lincoln explained his position on slavery. "I have no purpose, directly or indirectly to interfere with the institution of slavery in the states where it exists," he said. "I believe I have no lawful right to do so, and I have no inclination to do so."

Even though Lincoln didn't plan to interfere with slavery in the South, that didn't mean he supported it. "If slavery is not wrong, nothing is wrong," he once said. Lincoln's main concern was to keep the Union together and avoid a war. "My paramount object in this struggle is to save the Union, and is not to save or destroy slavery," Lincoln wrote. "If I could save the Union without freeing any slave, I would do it; and if I could save it by freeing all the slaves, I would do it;

and if I could do it by freeing some and leaving others alone, I would also do that."

But his words weren't enough to convince the South. Before the election southern leaders decided that the South would secede from the United States if Lincoln were elected.

South Carolina voted to leave the Union in December 1860. Alabama, Florida, Georgia, Louisiana, and Mississippi followed a month later. Texas seceded in February. These states formed the Confederate States of America. They elected former senator Jefferson Davis as their president. In time Virginia, North Carolina, Arkansas, and Tennessee also left the Union and joined the Confederacy.

Tensions were high throughout the country. The divided country couldn't exist forever. Something had to give, and it did. Confederate soldiers attacked Fort Sumter in Charleston, South Carolina, on April 12, 1861. The Civil War had begun.

It wasn't long before the war affected the Stowe family. Their 21-year-old son Frederick decided to

The bombardment of Fort Sumter was the beginning of the Civil War.

leave college to fight for the Union. Stowe worried about her son's safety but allowed him to go. She wrote to one of her daughters about the decision:

> *"Ever since war was declared which is now about two weeks—a little over—I have been like a person struggling in a nightmare dream. Fred immediately wanted to go, and I was willing he should if he could only get a situation where he could do any good. … Fred and I had a long talk Sunday night and he said he was willing to lay down his life for the*

cause and that if he died he felt he should go to the pure and good he had always longed for, and he and I kneeled down hand in hand and prayed for each other."

Stowe hadn't wanted her country to go to war. But since it had, she wanted the slaves to be freed as soon as possible. To her, that was even more important than saving the Union. This position put her at odds with President Lincoln, who wanted more than anything to restore the Union.

Both northerners and southerners believed that they would quickly win the war. They were both wrong. The Confederacy easily won the war's first battle, Bull Run, on July 21, 1861. For the next two years, the South won more battles than the North. But they came at a greater cost, since the South's population was much smaller than the North's.

In 1862 Congress passed a law that freed all Confederate slaves who agreed to fight for the Union. By then had Lincoln decided it would be necessary to free the slaves, but he gave the Confederate states one more chance. Lincoln issued a warning to the Confederate states on September 22, 1862. If they didn't return to the Union by January 1, 1863, he would free all slaves in the southern states.

Stowe was also upset about news that she was hearing from Great Britain. The British government and most of its

A MOUNTAIN OF MAIL

During the Civil War, Harriet received even more mail than she had before. She hired two full-time secretaries to help her answer the letters.

people were now supporting the Confederacy. British newspapers said the southern states had as much right to rebel as the original 13 American colonies had. Stowe was horrified that the people who had welcomed her so warmly just a few years earlier were on the South's side. To her, supporting the South meant that they were in favor of slavery.

At the time cotton mills were Britain's main industry. The mills needed southern cotton in order to produce cotton cloth. If the British government didn't trade with the Confederacy, the mills could close and put many people out of work. Britain also depended on trade with northern states. The Civil War interrupted that trade.

Much was riding on Britain's decision. If the British government officially recognized the Confederacy, the Union would have been forced to declare war on Great Britain as well. Even worse, French leaders hinted they would go along with whatever Great Britain did. The Union couldn't have managed to fight a war both at home and in Europe.

The British government hadn't yet officially recognized the Confederate government. Stowe wanted to do whatever she could to keep that from happening. She still had the 26 volumes of signatures from women of Great Britain who were against slavery. She planned to write a magazine article directed at the women, asking them to speak out against the Confederacy. But before she did that, she wanted to make sure that Lincoln planned to free all the slaves. She could then include this information in the article to support her position.

Harriet Beecher Stowe posed for a studio portrait.

Stowe decided to go to Washington and talk to
Lincoln. She traveled to Washington with her sister
Isabella and daughter Hattie in November 1862.

Lincoln's wife, Mary Todd Lincoln, invited Stowe to meet her husband at a tea at the White House on December 2. Massachusetts Senator Henry Wilson and his wife were also invited. No one knows exactly what Lincoln and Stowe talked about at the tea. But on January 1, 1863, Lincoln issued the Emancipation Proclamation. It freed all the slaves in the Confederate states. That day Calvin and Harriet were at a concert at the Boston Music Hall. When the crowd realized Stowe was there, they chanted her name until she stood up. Harriet listened to the crowd's applause with tears in her eyes.

Not everyone was pleased with the Emancipation Proclamation, though. Many people involved in the antislavery movement thought it didn't go far enough. It freed slaves only in the states that had seceded from the Union. Slavery remained legal in the border states of Delaware, Maryland, Kentucky, and Missouri.

Stowe wrote her article, which was printed in the January issue of *The Atlantic Monthly* magazine. She discussed what the Emancipation Proclamation meant

LINCOLN AND HARRIET

After Stowe met with President Lincoln at the White House, it was said that Lincoln greeted her by saying, "So you're the little lady who wrote the book that started this great war." However, there's no written evidence from either Lincoln or Stowe that he ever said those words. It may have been a family story that was repeated so often that people came to believe it was true.

and scolded British women for supporting the South. She reminded them of the petitions against slavery that so many of them had signed just 10 years before. She wrote: "We appeal to you as sisters, as wives, as mothers, to raise your voices to your fellow citizens, and your prayers to God for the removal of this affliction and disgrace from the Christian world."

Meanwhile, her brother Henry traveled to Great Britain for a speaking tour. He asked the British people to support the North and the antislavery cause. He often included quotes from Harriet's antislavery articles in his speeches.

Great Britain never recognized the Confederacy. Lincoln later said he believed this was because of *Uncle Tom's Cabin,* Harriet's article in *The Atlantic Monthly,* and Henry Ward Beecher's speaking tour.

A freedwoman from Philadelphia read Uncle Tom's Cabin *at a gathering in London, England.*

Union General William T. Sherman (right, leaning on cannon) with his staff in late 1864

Chapter Eight

REUNITING
A DIVIDED
COUNTRY

The Battle of Gettysburg in 1863 was the turning point of the war. From then on the Union Army won most of the battles. But even so, the war continued until 1865. Confederate General Robert E. Lee surrendered to Union General Ulysses S. Grant in the village of Appomattox Court House, Virginia, on April 9. President Lincoln urged both northerners and southerners to set aside their differences and move forward as one.

Just five days later, Confederate supporter John Wilkes Booth shot Lincoln at the Ford Theatre in Washington, D.C. Lincoln died the next morning. Many northerners wanted revenge for Lincoln's death as well as all the lives lost in the Civil War. But most remembered Lincoln's words urging the country to reunite. Although things were tense between the North and South for years, there were no large outbreaks of violence.

Stowe agreed with Lincoln. She was among the first people in the North to call for compassionate treatment for the South and its people. She believed that defeat in the war and the end of slavery were enough of a punishment.

Most of the Civil War had been fought on southern soil. The South was left shattered. Several of its largest cities were nearly destroyed. Its shipping and railroad systems were heavily damaged. Government leaders had to find a way to rebuild the South. They also had to agree on how the 11 states that had seceded from the Union would rejoin the country.

Vice President Andrew Johnson became president after Lincoln's death. Johnson's plan to rebuild the

A funeral train carried President Lincoln's body from Washington, D.C., to Illinois.

South was called Reconstruction. Johnson said all white people in the South should be pardoned. The southern states would form new state governments that had to outlaw slavery. Officials of the new governments had to swear loyalty to the United States. Once a state completed the steps, it would be allowed back in the Union. By 1870 the Union was once again complete.

Much of Richmond, Virginia, was in ruins after fire roared through the Confederate capital during the final days of the Civil War.

Most southerners were unhappy about the Reconstruction plan. But Stowe believed it was fair. Stowe traveled to the South several times after the Civil War ended. She was sad to see the destruction the war had left behind. She wrote to a friend: "I wish you could know of the sorrow and suffering I see, among people that one cannot help pitying. Yet a brighter day is breaking for both white and black."

A LOST SON

Frederick Stowe's life was difficult. He was an intelligent, mischievous child who often got into trouble. In his teens he began to drink alcohol heavily. His family sent him to take a "water cure" at a spa in New York, but it didn't help. He was attending medical school at Harvard University when he enlisted in the Union Army.

Fred did well in the army, reaching the rank of captain. In July 1863 he was wounded in the right ear at the bloody Battle of Gettysburg in Pennsylvania. Fred spent three months in a military hospital as his wound healed. He then was honorably discharged from the army and returned home.

The war had changed Fred for the worse. He was deaf in his wounded ear and had severe headaches. The pain caused him to become addicted to the painkiller morphine, as well as alcohol. His parents tried many times to help him, but nothing worked.

Fred traveled to California to find work on a ship in 1870. He was never heard from again. It's thought that he died shortly after arriving in California, but no one knows for sure. Harriet never lost hope that she would see her son again, but she died without knowing what happened to him.

On one trip Stowe visited the Confederate war memorial in Savannah, Georgia. She had always hoped the country could peacefully end slavery. She was sad that so many people lost their lives in a long, bloody war. But she believed that the country, both North and South, had brought this suffering on itself. Stowe thought God had sent the war to punish the United States for ignoring the slavery issue for so long.

Slavery officially ended when the U.S. Congress ratified the 13th Amendment to the Constitution in 1865. But Stowe knew that the end of slavery didn't mean the end of her work. She realized the newly freed blacks would face many difficulties. She was determined to do whatever she could to help them.

Stowe also tried to help her son Frederick turn his life around. She bought a former cotton plantation in Florida called Laurel Grove. She planned that Fred would help manage the plantation, and she and Calvin would live there in the winter. The plantation served as more than just something for Fred to do. It provided jobs for more than 100 former slaves. But after just

Frederick Stowe's life was never the same after the Civil War.

two years, Stowe realized that Fred wasn't working out as a manager. The plantation was losing money each month. The Stowes lost about $10,000 before selling the plantation.

In 1867 Stowe bought a 200-acre (80-hectare) orange grove in Mandarin, Florida. She gave Fred the job of managing the farm, but that job didn't suit him any better than the previous one. Still, Stowe kept the orange farm and became very involved in the Mandarin community. She helped start an Episcopal church, which also served as a school for former slaves.

In Florida Stowe saw black men become educated and buy property. She wrote: "An old Negro friend in our neighborhood has got a new, nice two-story house, and an orange grove, and a sugar mill. He has got a lot of money besides. Mr. Stowe met him one day, and he said, 'I have got 20 head of cattle, four head of 'hoss,' 40 head of hen, and I have got 10 children, all mine, every one mine.' Well, now, that is a thing that a black man could not say once, and this man was 60 years old before he could say it."

Both Calvin and Harriet loved Florida. In 1873 Harriet published *Palmetto Leaves,* a collection of sketches and essays about the state. The bestselling book sparked readers' interest in visiting and living in Florida. By the following year, land prices in the Mandarin area had doubled because of the demand.

Harriet (second from right) sat next to her husband, Calvin, at their home in Florida.

Florida newspapers gave Stowe credit for turning Florida into a winter vacation spot for northerners. Railroads offered expanded services to Florida from northern cities in the winter months. Stowe's book helped develop Florida's tourism industry, which remains strong today.

Southerners watched Stowe and the work she did. Among them was former Confederate General Robert E. Lee, who publicly praised Stowe's efforts to help the South. Gradually, southerners came to accept her.

Harriet Beecher Stowe accomplished great things during her long life.

chapter nine

THE FINAL YEARS

After the war Harriet Beecher Stowe's life became more settled and comfortable. The family had moved from Andover to Hartford, Connecticut, in 1864. There they built a large home in a neighborhood known as Nook Farm. Their neighbors included writers Mark Twain and Charles Dudley Warner, actor William Gillette, and Harriet's sister Isabella and her husband.

Stowe was never a big fan of speaking in public. But despite all the money she earned, she tended to spend it just as fast, mainly on other people. In 1872 the 61-year-old Stowe agreed to go on a speaking tour. She traveled throughout New England reading passages from some of her most popular books. At first Stowe was shy about speaking in front of an audience. As the tour went on, though, she became more comfortable. Her lectures sold out everywhere she went.

Stowe traveled from city to city by train. The food was bad, and the hotels she stayed in were often run-down. Even so, she enjoyed the tour. "I never sleep better than after a long day's ride," she said. The first tour went so well that she agreed to do another lecture tour in the Midwest the next year.

Along with giving lectures, Stowe continued to write. For the past 30 years, she had written a book nearly every year. She published her last book, *Poganuc People*, in 1878. She based the novel on her experiences growing up in Litchfield, Connecticut. She also wrote poems, magazine articles, children's stories, and essays. But none of these works ever became as successful as *Uncle Tom's Cabin*.

HARRIET'S CHILDREN

Stowe was proud of all of her children and loved them a great deal. But they also caused her sadness. Only three of them outlived her—the two oldest, Harriet and Eliza, and the youngest, Charley. Harriet and Eliza never married. They lived with their parents and cared for them in their old age. Charley became a minister. In 1911, with his son, Lyman, he published a biography of his mother 100 years after her birth.

Georgianna Stowe provided part of the inspiration for the character Topsy in her mother's famous book.

Just as in her winter home in Florida, Stowe became active in the Hartford community. She rediscovered her early interest in art and produced a number of oil paintings. Stowe helped revitalize the local art museum and started an art school that eventually became the University of Hartford.

Stowe was an international celebrity. Her circle of friends included famous authors such as Mark Twain and Oliver Wendell Holmes Senior, as well as members of the European nobility. But Stowe didn't let her fame go to her head. She remained a modest person who thought herself no better than anyone else.

In their later years Calvin and Harriet's marriage became more relaxed. They worried less about money because their oldest daughters took over managing the household and its expenses. Calvin hallucinated more as he got older, but his mind otherwise stayed sharp. Harriet was at his side when he died August 22, 1886, at age 85.

NOOK FARM

The Nook Farm neighborhood of Hartford began in 1853 when Harriet's brother-in-law John Hooker and his business partner bought 140 acres (57 hectares) near a nook in the Park River. The people who bought land from them and built houses in the neighborhood were a mixture of well-known writers, politicians, artists, and reformers of the day.

The Stowe house in Hartford was built in 1871.

They included Harriet's sister Isabella Beecher Hooker, who was active in the women's suffrage movement. Writer Mark Twain's house and the Stowe home still stand in Nook Farm. Twain's house is now the Mark Twain House and Museum. Harriet and Calvin's home is now part of the Harriet Beecher Stowe Center. Both homes are open to the public.

During her later years, Stowe may have had several strokes. Even in her youth, her memory was poor. Now her mind often wandered. She spent her days looking through picture books, picking flowers, and going on walks with her nurse. On days when her mind was clear, Stowe often talked about *Uncle Tom's Cabin.*

Just before midnight July 1, 1896, Harriet Beecher Stowe died at age 85. She was buried between her husband and her son Henry in the Andover Chapel Cemetery in Massachusetts.

At her funeral, beautiful bouquets of flowers stood along the sides of Stowe's grave. On top of her casket lay a very special wreath. The card attached to the wreath said: "The Children of Uncle Tom."

Harriet Beecher Stowe's famous novel Uncle Tom's Cabin *secured her place in history.*

Timeline

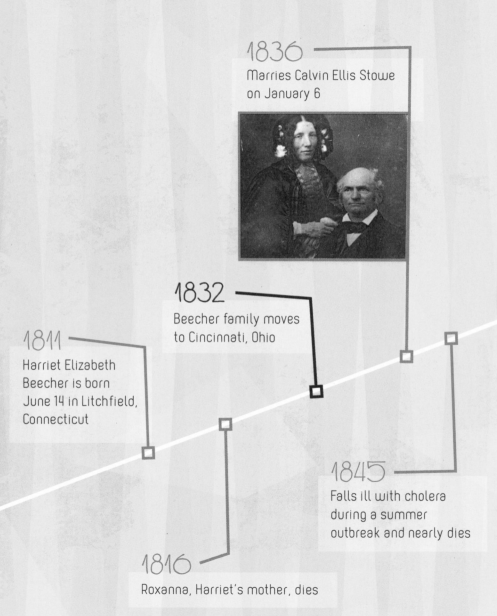

1836
Marries Calvin Ellis Stowe on January 6

1832
Beecher family moves to Cincinnati, Ohio

1811
Harriet Elizabeth Beecher is born June 14 in Litchfield, Connecticut

1845
Falls ill with cholera during a summer outbreak and nearly dies

1816
Roxanna, Harriet's mother, dies

1851
Uncle Tom's Cabin is printed in the *National Era* newspaper beginning June 5

1849
The Stowes' infant son Charley dies of cholera

1846
Recovers her health after visiting a spa in Brattleboro, Vermont

1850
The Stowes move to Maine, where Harriet writes *Uncle Tom's Cabin*

Timeline

1863

On January 1 President Abraham Lincoln issues the Emancipation Proclamation; shortly after, Stowe publishes an article asking British women to make sure Great Britain doesn't recognize the Confederacy

1852

Uncle Tom's Cabin is published in book form in March; the Stowes move to Andover, Massachusetts

1856

Returns to Europe

1853

Makes first trip to Europe; *The Key to Uncle Tom's Cabin* is published to back up materials found in Stowe's first book

1886
Calvin dies August 22

1872
Reads passages from her books during a lecture tour of New England

1873
Palmetto Leaves is published and helps make Florida a popular destination for travelers

1867
Buys an orange grove in Florida

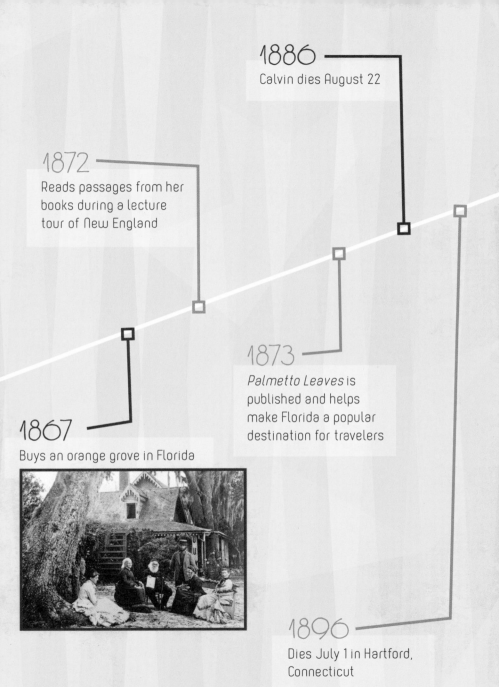

1896
Dies July 1 in Hartford, Connecticut

Glossary

abolitionists—people who supported the banning of slavery

cholera—dangerous disease that causes severe sickness and diarrhea

controversial—causing dispute or disagreement

emancipation—freedom from slavery or control

petition—letter signed by many people asking leaders for a change

philosophy—the study of truth, wisdom, and reality

radical—extreme compared to what most people think or do

Reconstruction—period following the Civil War, from 1865 to 1877, when the federal government controlled states in the former Confederacy and granted rights to African-Americans

royalty—a payment to an author for each copy of a book sold

secede—withdraw from

seminary—school where students are trained to become ministers or priests

tuberculosis—disease that affects the lungs and causes fever, cough, and difficulty breathing

OTHER BOOKS IN THIS SERIES

Further Reading

Gold, Susan Dudley. *The Women's Rights Movement and Abolitionism.*
New York: Cavendish Square Publishing, 2016.

Morretta, Alison. *Harriet Beecher Stowe and the Abolitionist Movement.*
New York: Cavendish Square Publishing, 2015.

Senker, Cath. *Who Traveled the Underground Railroad?*
Chicago: Capstone Heinemann Library, 2014.

Yancey, Diane. *The Abolition of Slavery.*
San Diego: ReferencePoint Press, 2013.

Internet Sites

Use FactHound to find Internet sites related to this book. All of
the sites on FactHound have been researched by our staff.

Here's all you do:

Visit www.facthound.com

Type in this code: 9780756551643

Source Notes

Page 11, line 1: Joan D. Hedrick. *Harriet Beecher Stowe: A Life.* New York: Oxford University Press, 1994, p. 207.

Page 11, line 5: Ibid.

Page 14, line 14: Edward Wagenknecht. *Harriet Beecher Stowe: The Known and the Unknown.* New York: Oxford University Press, 1965, p. 22.

Page 16, line 12: Johanna Johnston. *Runaway to Heaven: The Story of Harriet Beecher Stowe and Her Era.* Garden City, N.Y.: Doubleday, 1963, p. 5.

Page 17, line 3: Susan Belasco, ed. *Stowe in Her Own Time: A Biographical Chronicle Of Her Life, Drawn From Recollections, Interviews, and Memoirs by Family, Friends, and Associates.* Iowa City: University of Iowa Press, 2009, p. 11.

Page 20, line 17: Charles Edward Stowe and Lyman Beecher Stowe. *Harriet Beecher Stowe: The Story of Her Life.* Boston and New York: Houghton Mifflin Company, 1911, p. 28.

Page 32, line 1: *Harriet Beecher Stowe: A Life*, p. 136.

Page 32, line 5: Ibid., p. 119.

Page 34, line 8: *Harriet Beecher Stowe: The Known and the Unknown*, p. 93.

Page 37, line 6: *Runaway to Heaven: The Story of Harriet Beecher Stowe and Her Era*, p. 176.

Page 42, line 8: *Harriet Beecher Stowe: The Story of Her Life*, pp. 145–146.

Page 42, line 11: *Runaway to Heaven: The Story of Harriet Beecher Stowe and Her Era*, p. 203.

Page 43, line 4: Ibid.

Page 48, line 4: *Harriet Beecher Stowe: The Known and the Unknown*, p. 183.

Page 53, line 7: *Runaway to Heaven: The Story of Harriet Beecher Stowe and Her Era*, p. 263.

Page 57, line 5: *Harriet Beecher Stowe: The Story of Her Life*, p. 165.

Page 62, line 6: *Harriet Beecher Stowe: The Known and the Unknown*, p. 166.

Page 64, line 1: Ibid., p. 89.

Page 64, sidebar, line 6: Charles Edward Stowe. *Life of Harriet Beecher Stowe, Compiled From Her Letters and Journals*. Boston, New York: Houghton, Mifflin and Company, 1891, p. 235.

Page 73, line 9: The Avalon Project: First Inaugural Address of Abraham Lincoln. March 4, 1861. 31 Dec. 2015. http://avalon. law.yale.edu/19th_century/lincoln1.asp

Page 73, line 15: "If Slavery Is Not Wrong, Nothing is Wrong (Top Treasures)." American Treasures of the Library of Congress. 31 Dec. 2015. https://www.loc.gov/exhibits/treasures/trt027.html

Page 73, line 17: *Runaway to Heaven: The Story of Harriet Beecher Stowe and Her Era*, p. 354.

Page 75, line 4: *Harriet Beecher Stowe: The Known and the Unknown*, p. 67.

Page 81, line 3: *Harriet Beecher Stowe: A Life*, p. vii.

Page 82, line 4: *Harriet Beecher Stowe: The Known and the Unknown*, p. 358.

Page 88, line 6: *Runaway to Heaven: The Story of Harriet Beecher Stowe and Her Era*, p. 389.

Page 92, line 7: *Harriet Beecher Stowe: The Story of Her Life*, p. 227.

Page 96, line 9: David McCullough. *Brave Companions: Portraits in History*. New York: Prentice Hall Press, 1992, p. 50.

Select Bibliography

Adams, John R. *Harriet Beecher Stowe*. New York: Twayne Publishers, 1963.

The Avalon Project: First Inaugural Address of Abraham Lincoln. March 4, 1861. 31 Dec. 2015. http://avalon.law.yale.edu/19th_century/lincoln1.asp

Belasco, Susan, ed. *Stowe in Her Own Time: A Biographical Chronicle Of Her Life, Drawn From Recollections, Interviews, and Memoirs by Family, Friends, and Associates.* Iowa City: University of Iowa Press, 2009.

Downs, Robert B., et al. *Memorable Americans: 1750-1950.* Littleton, Colo.: Libraries Unlimited, 1983.

Gerson, Noel B. *Harriet Beecher Stowe*. New York: Praeger Publishers, 1976.

Hedrick, Joan D. *Harriet Beecher Stowe: A Life.* New York: Oxford University Press, 1994.

Hillstrom, Kevin, and Laurie Collier Hillstrom. *American Civil War Almanac.* Detroit: UXL, 2000.

Hillstrom, Kevin, and Laurie Collier Hillstrom. *American Civil War Biographies.* Vol. I-II. Detroit: UXL, 2000.

"If Slavery Is Not Wrong, Nothing is Wrong" (Top Treasures). American Treasures of the Library of Congress. 31 Dec. 2015. https://www.loc.gov/exhibits/treasures/trt027.html

Johnston, Johanna. *Runaway to Heaven: The Story of Harriet Beecher Stowe and Her Era.* Garden City, N.Y.: Doubleday, 1963.

McCullough, David. *Brave Companions: Portraits in History.* New York: Prentice Hall Press, 1992.

McHenry, Robert. *Famous American Women: A Biographical Dictionary from Colonial Times to the Present.* New York: Dover, 1983.

Stoddard, Hope. *Famous American Women*. New York: Crowell, 1970.

Stowe, Charles Edward. *Life of Harriet Beecher Stowe, Compiled From Her Letters and Journals.* Boston, New York: Houghton, Mifflin and Company, 1891.

Stowe, Charles Edward, and Lyman Beecher Stowe. *Harriet Beecher Stowe: The Story of Her Life.* Boston: Houghton Mifflin, 1911.

Stowe, Harriet Beecher. *Uncle Tom's Cabin.* Boston: John P. Jewett & Co., 1852.

Wagenknecht, Edward. *Harriet Beecher Stowe: The Known and the Unknown.* New York: Oxford University Press, 1965.

White, Hilda. *Truth Is My Country: Portraits of Eight New England Authors.* Garden City, N.Y.: Doubleday, 1971.

Index

Index cont.

CRITICAL THINKING USING THE COMMON CORE

1. In addition to her writing, how did Harriet Beecher Stowe work to improve the lives of both black and white Americans? Use evidence from the text to support your answer. (Key Ideas and Details)

2. Harriet's father once said that he would give $100 if she could have been born a boy. What did he mean by that? How have attitudes toward men and women changed since Stowe's time? (Integration of Knowledge and Ideas)

3. *Uncle Tom's Cabin* was credited by many people, including President Lincoln, as contributing to the start of the Civil War. What would it have been like to write such an influential book? (Integration of Knowledge and Ideas)